PIGNAF

THE STORY OF PIPPA'S TRANSITION FROM FACTORY FARM TO FAMILY FARM

Instructions:

- Choose your favorite reading spot, such as a beanbag chair, comfy desk, or under your favorite oak tree. Be sure to have colored pencils, pens, or markers ready to doodle and practice your art skills.
- If you are using the book for school, work on one page a day, or as many as you want to fit into your curriculum. Each section contains a segment of the story, a coloring page, vocabulary page, and an activity page.
- Think of all the different ways to find information for the research pages. Have your parent help with any searches on the Internet or schedule a library day. The common definitions for the **112** vocabulary words are in the glossary in the back of the book.

"Let the field be joyful, and all that is in it. Then all the trees of the woods will rejoice before the LORD."
~Psalm 96:12 (NKJV)

The Thinking Tree Publishing Company, LLC
& Sarah Janisse Brown
Copyright 2016 — Do Not Copy — Dyslexie Font

Story by Mark Apple
Design/Edit/Activities by Nora Marie Apple
Illustrations/Artwork by Tolik Trishkin
Cover by Feodor Zubrytskyy

I GET TO LIVE LIKE A PIG?
CHAPTER ONE

Hi there. My name is **11021963**. Well, that was my given name when I was born. This is my story about the scariest day of my life, and the week that followed.

I was just lying in my crate, the only thing I had ever done besides eat and sleep. The men in the uniforms and badges had just brought me more corn meal, which was what we ate for every meal. I slopped it up. I do love to eat!

I was just lying there under the bright lights minding my own business, just thinking normal pig thoughts, such as:

In this big world of pigs, where there are pigs as far as I can see, why can't I play with any of them? Why do we just lie around all day? We eat, lie down, sleep, eat, lie down, sleep, over and over and over again. Why are the lights so bright? Sometimes when I'm sleepy, I think I would like it to be dark.

Why am I always alone even though I can see, and hear, and smell other pigs? Wouldn't it be fun to play?

I wonder ...

VOCABULARY WORDS

Use the glossary in the back of the book to find the meaning of each word or phrase:

factory farming _____

_____

organic farming _____

_____

crate _____

_____

concrete _____

_____

ACTIVITY: PERSPECTIVE
HOW MANY PIGS LIVE IN THIS INDUSTRIAL BARN? ____

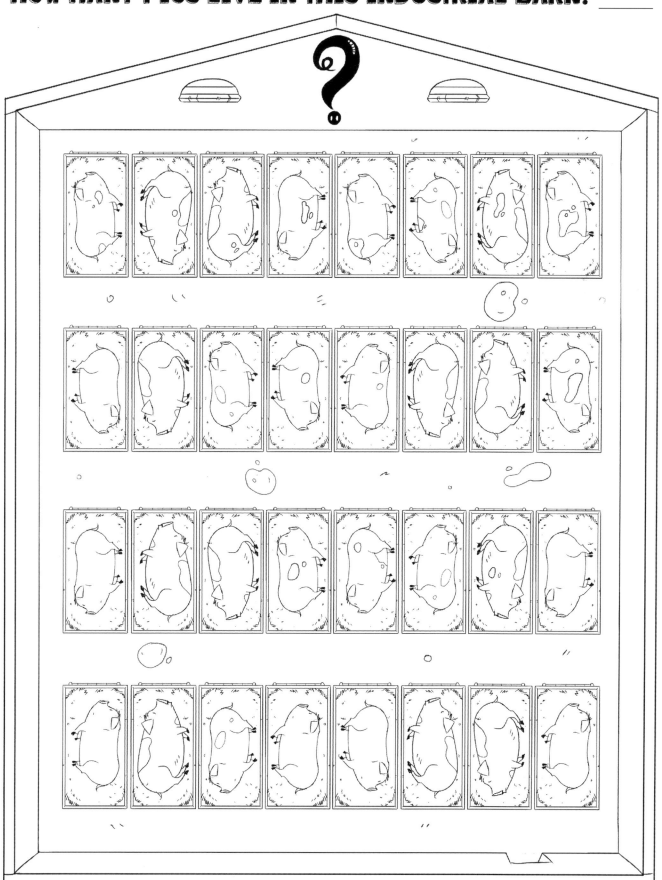

All of a sudden, an even brighter light was in my eyes, and two men were standing in the middle of the bright light. A man with a funny hat that I had never seen before nodded his head. Then he picked me up. He then started walking away, taking me away from the only other 'friends' that I knew, or kind of knew.

At least we could see one another...

He just kept walking, and walking, and walking. Past millions and billions of other pigs. Well, I don't really know how to count that high, so I don't really know how many. But he just kept walking all the way to the end of the world.

And then, he walked out of the world!

Well, I didn't know until then, that there is more to the world than just crates and crates and crates of pigs.

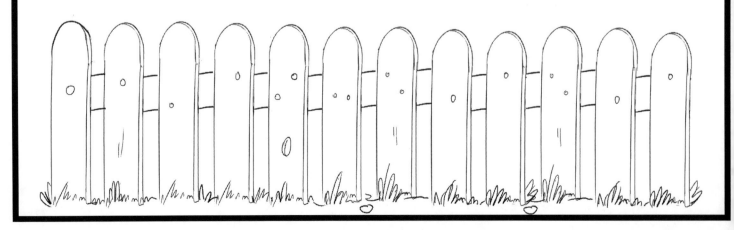

VOCABULARY WORDS

Use the glossary in the back of the book to find the meaning of each word or phrase:

fluorescent light _____

_____

natural light _____

_____

corn meal _____

_____

grains _____

_____

ACTIVITY: CAN YOU DRAW IT?
DRAW A PICTURE OF PIPPA IN AN INDUSTRIAL FARM:

The man with the funny hat said, "You're finally outside pig!" I was scared because this man seemed to be *pignapping* me from my home!

I could not believe what I was seeing. My heart was thumping. To see a blue sky made my eyes nearly pop out! I had always stared at the top of the silver sky, but this sky was so much bigger! And blue! With puffy looking white things I found out later are called clouds!

I could see all kinds of new things in this big new world.

At the end of the concrete floor there were tiny green sticks that stretched to the beginning of the big blue sky! I had never seen so many beautiful colors! Well, I later found out it was grass, but it looked like sticks! Out of the little green sticks were large brown sticks that reached to the sky. They had big flat green papers on the ends that made the ground much cooler with its shade! Later, I found out the big brown sticks were called trees.

I did not understand this big new world!

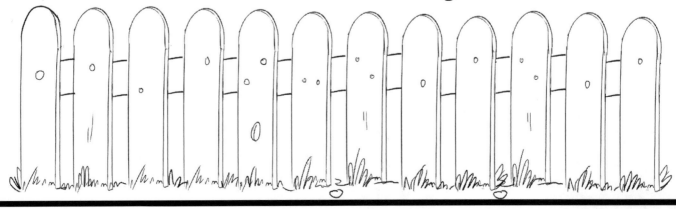

VOCABULARY WORDS

Use the glossary in the back of the book to find the meaning of each word or phrase:

agriculture _____

_____

homestead _____

_____

barn _____

_____

tractor _____

_____

ACTIVITY: DRAW THE MISSING PARTS:

Then the man with the funny hat put me into a bigger crate. He got inside the big crate through another door. All of a sudden, the crate started to roar! Then the big crate started moving!

The moving crate was not like my small crate in my silver home. In my old crate, I could never turn around to see out the back. The moving crate was so big I could turn around and see everywhere!

I heard the man call the moving crate a farm truck.

I guess the man saw how scared I was, because he just smiled, and said "it's ok, pig, we'll be home soon." I did not yet know what that meant.

What was going to happen to me?

The man's voice sounded so kind that I felt safe. I felt calmer as I watched this new world in the moving truck. I was surprised at all the beautiful colors!

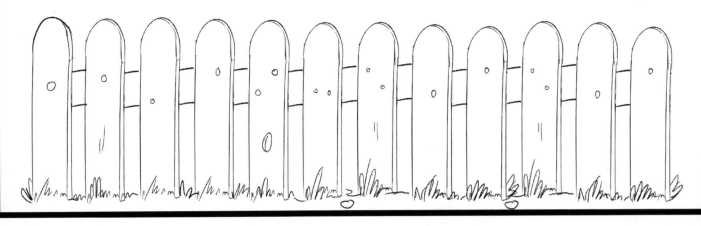

VOCABULARY WORDS

Use the glossary in the back of the book to find the meaning of each word or phrase:

pig _____

_____

boar _____

_____

hog _____

_____

sow _____

_____

ACTIVITY: RESEARCH PAGE

RESEARCH THE DIFFERENCE BETWEEN FLUORESCENT AND NATURAL LIGHTS. TELL HOW EACH LIGHT AFFECTS THE ANIMALS' GROWTH:

All of a sudden, the farm truck stopped. Then the farm truck was silent. Then the man with the funny hat got out of the farm truck and shouted: "we're home!"

When he lifted me out of the moving crate, more people of different sizes came running to us. The smallest ones were noisy and grabbing me. It scared me. I was thinking that maybe I should go back to where I came from. However, soon I could tell that they liked me!

They were petting me!

One of them broke off part of what she was eating and put it in my face. It was not corn meal. I was feeling hungry so I took a bite. She said it was bread.

It was so tasty and different from the corn meal!

It is my favorite thing to eat now. They were all playing with me at the same time! I went from being very frightened to having fun.

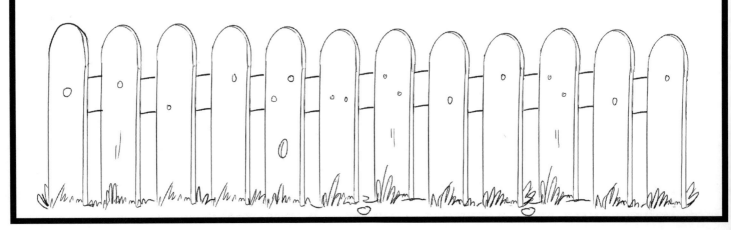

VOCABULARY WORDS

Use the glossary in the back of the book to find the meaning of each word or phrase:

excited _____

_____

harvest _____

_____

acorn _____

_____

ranch _____

_____

ACTIVITY: CAN YOU DRAW IT?

DRAW A PICTURE OF PIPPA ON A HOMESTEAD FARM:

The man with the funny hat said, "This is my farm. This is your new home!" I was so excited to learn the man with the funny hat was a Farmer and I was going to live on a *real* farm!

Then he asked the smaller people, "What shall we name her?" The littlest one said, "How about, um, hmmm ... Pippa, Pippa the Pig!" Everyone started laughing and cheering: "Pippa it is!

From now on, you are Pippa the Pig!"

You can forget about my old name: **11021963**, they never use it.

What is your name?

Hello! My Name Is

_____

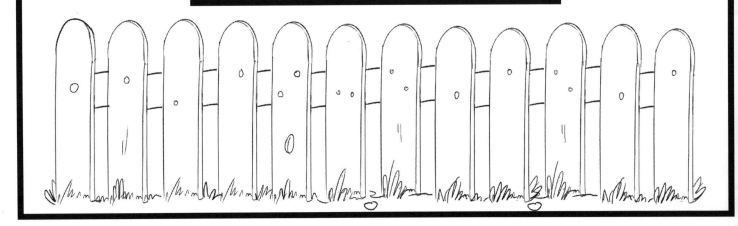

VOCABULARY WORDS

Use the glossary in the back of the book to find the meaning of each word or phrase:

irrigate _____

_____

ground water _____

_____

manure _____

_____

4H _____

_____

ACTIVITY: DRAW THE MISSING PARTS:

After playing with the children for a long time, I started getting sleepy; so sleepy that I could barely keep my eyes open. The sky was no longer blue. It started changing into orange and purple. At least that is what someone said. The Farmer with the funny hat said, "I see it's time to take Pippa to where she will sleep, she's had a big day." They took me through a gate that had lots of grass!

I had never walked in grass!

It was not only nice to look at and walk in; it also tasted wonderful! Grass is my favorite thing to eat now. And there were lots of acorns on the ground under the trees! They are now my favorite thing to eat! Even more than the grass! And the bread.

Inside the gate, there was a little shelter with lots of straw in it for me to lie in. My new straw bed is much more cozy and comfortable than my old bed in the crate with the concrete floor.

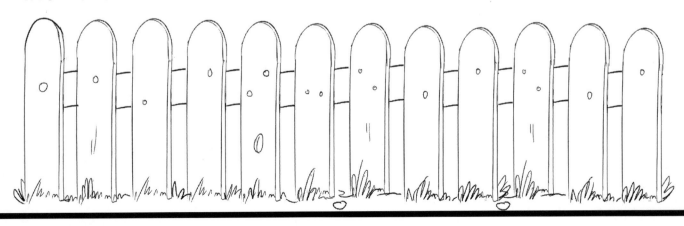

VOCABULARY WORDS

Use the glossary in the back of the book to find the meaning of each word or phrase:

explore _____

_____

protect _____

_____

fence _____

_____

gate _____

_____

ACTIVITY: RESEARCH PAGE
RESEARCH THE SLEEPING HABITS OF SWINE.
TELL HOW PROPER BEDDING BENEFITS THE PIG'S HEALTH:

As I lay down in the fresh straw, I looked to the far end of the grass and saw the funniest looking pigs I had ever seen! They were walking on two legs, up a plank, going into their home to sleep! A boy shut the door behind them. I could not wait until they came back out so I could play with them!

The Farmer with the funny hat said:

"Pippa, from now on, you are a pig that gets to *live* like a pig."

Then, all of a sudden I realized the light was fading, it really does get dark when it is time to sleep.

Oh, I started my story by telling you that this was the *scariest* day of my life. It was only scary at first.

It turned out that this was the *best* day of my life!

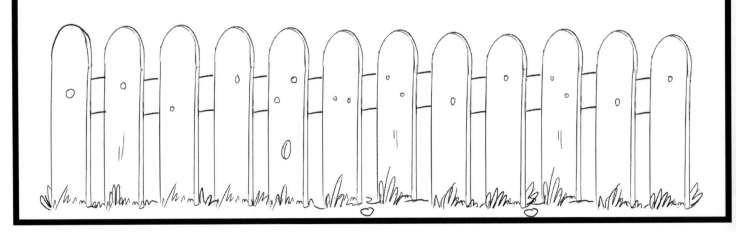

ESSAY

Write a paragraph about the type of farm you would create:

_____

_____

_____

_____

_____

_____

_____

_____

_____

_____

_____

ACTIVITY: CAN YOU DRAW IT?
DRAW A PICTURE OF A MOBILE HEN HOUSE:

BUT THEN I MET ROBBIE, THE ROOSTER

CHAPTER TWO

It turns out that those two-legged pigs that walked the plank at bedtime were not really pigs after all.

I was so excited to explore my new home, the farm, that I was the first one up after the light came back on (it is called the sun). I decided to wait by their door for them to come out.

As soon as their little door opened, I was there to greet them. Well, the first one out was not as excited to see me as I was to see him! He began squawking and bouncing around and flapping what turned out to be wings, and charged right at me!

I was not sure exactly what he actually said, but I *am* sure that it would not be appropriate to print in this book.

I only wanted to be friends!

VOCABULARY WORDS

Use the glossary in the back of the book to find the meaning of each word or phrase:

rooster _____

_____

squawk _____

_____

mobile hen house _____

_____

plank _____

_____

ACTIVITY: DRAW THE MISSING PARTS:

What I have now learned, is that those funny feathery creatures are called chickens. The noisy one is a boy, called a rooster.

Robbie is his name.

I call him Mean Robbie sometimes. The rest of the chickens are girls, called hens. They are all very nice, not like Mean Robbie. They mostly just walk around all day, bobbing their heads, and making me laugh.

They almost *never* stop talking.

The hens that live on my new farm are always happy and love to sing. They dance and run around the field all day! In my old home we were never allowed to walk out of our crates. I wonder what their old home was like.

I wonder if they lived in crates too.

VOCABULARY WORDS

Use the glossary in the back of the book to find the meaning of each word or phrase:

chicken _____

_____

hen _____

_____

pasture raised _____

_____

free-range _____

_____

ACTIVITY: RESEARCH PAGE

RESEARCH THE MOBILE CHICKEN COOP AND BATTERY FARMS. DESCRIBE THE DIFFERENCE IN THE HEALTH OF THE CHICKEN AND THE QUALITY IN THE EGGS:

~MOBILE CHICKEN COOP~

~BATTERY FARMS~

The chickens like to eat bugs, grass, and seeds.

When one finds a bug, they chase each other around trying to take it away.

The best thing about the hens are that they make the most wonderful and delightful things called eggs. They are my favorite thing to eat now! Except for acorns, and bread, and grass, and grains. I am getting hungry thinking about eating!

I had never tasted a whole egg, but sometimes when they break, the little girls give them to me and tell me it is a gift from the chickens.

Eggs make me very happy.

I think the chickens are the real gift because they make eggs and make me happy watching them. Sometimes, when Robbie is not making me mad, I even remember that he is also a gift.

VOCABULARY WORDS

Use the glossary in the back of the book to find the meaning of each word or phrase:

poultry _____

_____

battery farm _____

_____

chicken coop _____

_____

hatchery _____

_____

ACTIVITY: CAN YOU DRAW IT?
DRAW A PICTURE OF A BATTERY FARM:

I am happy that I get to live like a pig.

I am happy that the hens get to live like hens. I am *trying* to like Robbie more.

Robbie is just protecting the hens, making sure they are safe.

That is why he is sometimes mean. He scares away anyone that might hurt the hens. Their eggs always taste better when they are happy and feel safe.

So, I guess Robbie is just doing what he is supposed to be doing.

After a full day of being entertained by the chickens, I decided that I would explore farther back behind my new home, but not until after I got some sleep.

ESSAY

Write a paragraph about the kinds of animals that would live on your farm:

_____

_____

_____

_____

_____

_____

_____

_____

_____

_____

_____

ACTIVITY: DRAW THE MISSING PARTS:

WHAT IS THAT?!

CHAPTER THREE

Day three of living on a real farm started with the surprise and shockingly loud and very strange song by my *'friend'* Robbie while I was still sleeping.

He sure has a loud voice.

I thought it was still time to sleep. But unlike yesterday, when I was so excited and the first one awake, Robbie was first, crowing at sunrise. And he wanted everyone to know it. He is *so* loud.

Robbie believes his job, besides protecting the hens, is to let everyone know it is time to get up for breakfast. At least, *almost* time.

Since I like to eat, I'm now happy for Robbie to wake us up.

VOCABULARY WORDS

Use the glossary in the back of the book to find the meaning of each word or phrase:

bovine _____

_____

bull _____

_____

cow _____

_____

heifer _____

_____

ACTIVITY: RESEARCH PAGE

RESEARCH GRASSFED BEEF AND FEEDLOT BEEF. DESCRIBE THE DIFFERENCE IN THE HEALTH OF THE CATTLE AND THE QUALITY IN THE BEEF AND MILK:

~GRASSFED BEEF~

~FEEDLOT BEEF~

After wandering the opposite way of the chicken coop, I started running. I realized that I love to run.

I had never run before, because in my crate at my old home, I could only move two steps.

Anyway, I was running around the corner of the barn when all of a sudden I ran into what looked like trees, but with feet like mine, except really, really, big!

I stepped back so that I could see to the top, and there was a **HUGE** black and white animal just standing there chewing something. She seemed to have barely noticed me as she just kept chewing. She was wearing a big necklace that had a big bell on it. It made a very pretty sound.

It turns out that is her name, Belle.

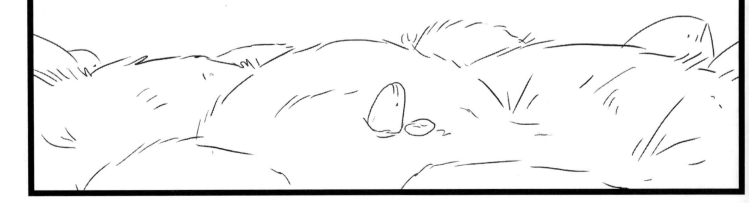

VOCABULARY WORDS

Use the glossary in the back of the book to find
the meaning of each word or phrase:

livestock _____

_____

feed lots _____

_____

industrial barn _____

_____

dairy cow _____

_____

ACTIVITY: PERSPECTIVE
DRAW COWS IN THE STALLS IN THIS INDUSTRIAL BARN

I found out that Belle and I have something in common. (Oh, yes, I forgot to mention that Belle is a cow, not a giant pig.) She came from a place much like where I came from. Apparently, where she is from, all the cows live in a metal barn together and barely have room to move. I see why Belle did not like that. Here at our new home, she moves from place to place in hay fields all day long.

Belle is a cow that now gets to live like a cow!

She loves grass, everything about grass. She loves to lay in grass, she loves to roll around in the grass, and she especially loves to eat grass and clover and alfalfa. I thought I loved to eat grass, but Belle *especially* loves to eat grass.

I do not think I have seen her eat anything else, she loves it so much..

VOCABULARY WORDS

Use the glossary in the back of the book to find the meaning of each word or phrase:

alfalfa _____

_____

haylage _____

_____

milk _____

_____

milking parlor _____

_____

ACTIVITY: CAN YOU DRAW IT?
DRAW A PICTURE OF BELLE EATING HER FAVORITE FOOD:

I like Belle. I like her because even though she is so big that I was scared of her at first, she is so nice. She is so calm that I feel very relaxed just watching her and being around her.

But my favorite thing about Belle is that I sometimes get a treat of my most favorite thing in the world: *milk*! Most evenings someone will bring a bucket of Belle's wonderful milk and pour it into my trough. They tell me that it is a gift from Belle. It tastes so wonderful, and makes me feel so good.

Did I already mention that milk is my favorite?

Along with acorns, and grass, and eggs, and grains and bread. Milk poured on top of the grains is especially my favorite!

Because Belle is so calm, and nice, and gives such wonderful milk, I think *Belle* is the real gift.

ESSAY

Write a paragraph about the kind of foods the animals eat in an industrial farm:

_____

_____

_____

_____

_____

_____

_____

_____

_____

_____

_____

ACTIVITY: DRAW THE MISSING PARTS:

DRAW A BELL ON BELLE:

ARE YOU KIDDING ME?
CHAPTER FOUR

As the next day began, day 4 of being at my new home on the farm, I thought that this would be a quiet day with nothing new to experience for a change.

I was wrong!

It seems that, although Belle loves to eat grass, there was a discussion about how she wasn't eating it fast enough and that thistles and other weeds were growing up and taking over the farm. The Farmer with the funny hat said he had an idea about how to take care of the problem.

He hopped into his big, loud farm truck and disappeared in a cloud of dust.

VOCABULARY WORDS

Use the glossary in the back of the book to find the meaning of each word or phrase:

experience _____

_____

discussion _____

_____

thistle _____

_____

weed _____

_____

ACTIVITY: RESEARCH

RESEARCH IRRIGATION. TELL HOW IRRIGATION BENEFITS PLANTS AND ANIMALS:

_____

_____

_____

_____

_____

CREATE (DRAW) A WAY THAT FOOD CAN BE GROWN IN VERY DRY OR ROCKY AREAS:

The rest of the day was mostly spent lazily watching the hens chase each other around the pasture, eating, and occasionally fighting with Robbie, for fun of course, then eating some more. Watching Belle trying to eat all the grass in the world made me hungry again, so we had lunch together!

Belle takes care of the grass when she eats, but the chickens pick and pull the grass down to the bare soil! The chickens live in a mobile hen house that the Farmer with the funny hat moves to a different pasture every day to give the grass time to grow back.

I found out that cows only have bottom teeth.

Belle can't eat the grass all the way down to the ground so it grows back much quicker. She chews her food a lot longer than anyone else I know! I was finished eating long before Belle. I sat and relaxed with her while she chewed.

Basically it was a quiet day, just as I expected. Until...

VOCABULARY WORDS

Use the glossary in the back of the book to find the meaning of each word or phrase:

hungry _____

_____

occasionally _____

_____

pesticide _____

_____

soil _____

_____

ACTIVITY: RESEARCH PAGE

RESEARCH ORGANIC CROP FARMING AND CONVENTIONAL CROP FARMING. DESCRIBE THE DIFFERENCE IN THE HEALTH OF THE SOIL AND THE QUALITY IN THE PLANTS:

~ORGANIC FARMING~

~CONVENTIONAL FARMING~

A roar and a cloud of dust appeared. The moving crate came home, well, I guess it's a farm truck. The family came running out of the house. They were all very excited and very noisy. Just like when I first came home.

The Farmer with the funny hat opened the back of the farm truck and out jumped funny looking creatures that had beards, and some had horns on top of their heads. One of the little girls said: "One ... two ... three ... four ... you brought *five* goats!"

We have five goats?!

Goats? What is a goat? They looked funny, a little bit like Belle, but closer to my size. I thought I could manage them if they caused me any trouble.

I don't know if I have ever been wrong about anything, but I was sure wrong about that!

VOCABULARY WORDS

Use the glossary in the back of the book to find the meaning of each word or phrase:

horn _____

_____

goat _____

_____

kid _____

_____

trouble _____

_____

ACTIVITY: CAN YOU DRAW IT?
DRAW A PICTURE OF A GOAT:

As soon as the children put them down, those goats were causing trouble. One went and stood right in the middle of my food trough, one was standing on my little house, and one with horns went right through a fence and got his head stuck.

But the two bigger goats, **Greta** and **Gracie**, saw some tall grass that Belle does not like and started eating. They ate it as though they loved it and could not get enough. They liked it so much that they didn't seem to notice that their **kids** were not behaving very well. The kids were going through the chicken house, causing the hens and Robbie to voice their opinions much more loudly than usual.

They were making a mess of my home!

I did not think I was going to like goats very much. The little ones were very naughty. Their names are **Garrett**, **Gabby**, and **George**.

VOCABULARY WORDS

Use the glossary in the back of the book to find the meaning of each word or phrase:

trough _____

_____

through _____

_____

opinion _____

_____

stressed _____

_____

ACTIVITY: DRAW THE MISSING PARTS:

But then, one of the boys put the big goats on a small table, and milked the goats, just like they milked Belle. Then he brought the bucket to my trough and said: "Here Pippa, you seem a little stressed."

"Here is a gift from Greta and Gracie."

It was so good! It made all the trouble of the little ones not seem so bad. The sky was just starting to look orange and purple again. I then saw where Greta and Gracie had been eating the tall weeds.

The field now looks so pretty!

Where did all those tall weeds go? The goats had eaten all those tall weeds! Now the sunsets are even prettier than they were before! Now I see that Greta, Gracie, and maybe even Garrett, Gabby, and George are the real gifts!

ESSAY

Write a paragraph about the kind of foods the animals eat on a natural farm:

_____

_____

_____

_____

_____

_____

_____

_____

_____

_____

ACTIVITY: RESEARCH PAGE

RESEARCH PESTICIDES. MAKE A LIST OF THE POSITIVE EFFECTS AND A LIST OF THE NEGATIVE EFFECTS OF PESTICIDES:

ACORNS AND CLOUDS
CHAPTER FIVE

As I awoke on day five, I realized how life here on this wonderful farm was going to be full of activity, never dull or boring.

Watching the busy-body hens made me happy.
Watching the new goats play made me happy.
Watching Belle eat always made me happy because I then always ate too, which also made me happy.

Even watching Robbie protect the hens made me happy.

The children came to see me every day and that made me really happy!

VOCABULARY WORDS

Use the glossary in the back of the book to find the meaning of each word or phrase:

activity _____

_____

wonderful _____

_____

everywhere _____

_____

buried _____

_____

ACTIVITY: CAN YOU DRAW IT?
DRAW A PICTURE OF A FOREST WITH DIFFERENT KINDS OF TREES, PLANTS, AND WEEDS:

On my fifth day at my real farm, they took me to their happy spot on the farm. They took turns carrying me through Belle's pasture. We had walked farther than I had ever gone on my own.

We finally got to a gate at the end of the pasture that led into a place full of trees. They set me down in a very soft place, full of leaves, with soft grass.

I noticed acorns, acorns everywhere, millions, billions of acorns!

I ate all that I could in that spot. Then I smelled some acorns that were buried in the ground, so I dug them with my nose. I realized how much I loved digging in the ground! It was my most favorite thing to do. Except for eating. I loved eating the grass, leaves, and acorns! And I loved that spot because it was so shady and cool. I loved the trees because of the acorns, and the shade, and the soft dirt to dig in.

It really was a happy spot!

VOCABULARY WORDS

Use the glossary in the back of the book to find the meaning of each word or phrase:

forest _____

_____

foliage _____

_____

farther _____

_____

field _____

_____

ACTIVITY: DRAW THE MISSING PARTS:

After the children finished their picnic, finished climbing trees, and finished playing, they decided it was time to go back. I did not think it was time because there were so many more acorns still to eat. But, one of them picked me up and we headed back.

As we were about half way through Belle's pasture, I wondered if I was awake or dreaming.

It seemed like there were a lot more goats than Greta, Gracie, Garrett, Gabby, and George.

I was not the only one that noticed; the children did too. They started walking faster and faster, then they were running from excitement. They put me on the ground, so I ran too.

VOCABULARY WORDS

Use the glossary in the back of the book to find the meaning of each word or phrase:

picnic _____

_____

seemed _____

_____

noticed _____

_____

dreaming _____

_____

ACTIVITY: RESEARCH PAGE

RESEARCH SHEARING SHEEP: LIST THE WAYS ANIMALS ARE USEFUL ON A FARM OTHER THAN BEING RAISED FOR FOOD:

When we got to the little pasture by the chicken coop and my house, I could not believe what I was seeing. All bunched up in the corner, were these animals that looked kind of like goats, but also kind of like clouds.

Clouds with legs, and heads!

With all the excitement of the children, they seemed very frightened. The children were trying to count them: "one... two... three... four... hey, stop moving so I can count!"

"One... two... three... I lost count *again*!" Another said: "There are eight, eight sheep!"

Sheep? What is a sheep?

VOCABULARY WORDS

Use the glossary in the back of the book to find the meaning of each word or phrase:

flock _____

_____

ram _____

_____

sheep _____

_____

ewe _____

_____

ACTIVITY: CAN YOU DRAW IT?
DRAW A PICTURE OF SHEEP:

The sheep seemed very nice, but shy. They were always together in a close group, always in a flock. They looked soft and cozy. After a while, they seemed to relax so I could join them.

I like the sheep.

There were big ones and little ones. Some were brown, and some were white.

They ate grass too!

I heard the Farmer with the funny hat say their hair would make warm clothes for the winter. It just looked like a mess to me! He said their hair is called wool, and they would shear the sheep and wash it first. I wondered if they would make a blanket for me.

They made the farm even nicer.

VOCABULARY WORDS

Use the glossary in the back of the book to find the meaning of each word or phrase:

wool _____

_____

shear _____

_____

howling _____

_____

coyote _____

_____

That night as I was just falling asleep, thinking about my new friends, I heard the scariest noise I had ever heard. Howling! Then more howling, but closer.

I started to feel a little scared, but just then the Farmer with the funny hat and the big boys came out of the house. I saw eyes in the dark, and could see them just a little off in the distance.

They said it was coyotes.

Apparently, it was very serious. One of the boys said he would spend the night protecting the sheep. I did not like being scared, but I felt safe that the boy was guarding us.

I decided I would stay up too. I wanted the sheep to be safe, so, just like the children earlier, I kept trying to count them. One, two, three, four, I started getting very, very sleepy. Five... six... seven..., Finally, I drifted... off... to... sl...

ESSAY

Write a paragraph about how farm animals pro-
vide more than just food:

_____

_____

_____

_____

_____

_____

_____

_____

_____

_____

ACTIVITY: RESEARCH PAGE
RESEARCH SILOS AND TELL ABOUT THEIR USE ON FARMS:

GONE TO THE DOGS
CHAPTER SIX

The next morning when I woke up, everything seemed normal, except there were more animals, and a lot more noises. Unlike the constant sounds of metal clanking on my old farm, the sounds on my new farm made me happy. Well, except for Robbie.

No matter who was new to the farm, Robbie did not seem to mind waking them up.

The chickens love to eat bugs and worms, and Robbie gets the first one every morning. Then he tells us all about it. He crows over and over and over again. He is very proud.

Every morning, I look forward to the Farmer with the funny hat coming out of his house. He saves yummy food from his breakfast and puts it in my trough to eat.

I love to eat healthy food!

VOCABULARY WORDS

Use the glossary in the back of the book to find the meaning of each word or phrase:

proud _____

_____

normal _____

_____

gathered _____

_____

breakfast _____

_____

ACTIVITY: CAN YOU DRAW IT?

DRAW A PICTURE OF SILOS ON A FARM:

The morning discussion was all about the coyotes. The bigger boys gathered tools and said they would make the fences better and stronger.

Even I knew the fences were not strong because the kids, Garrett, Gabby, and George, were always sneaking on the other side.

Fences never seem to discourage goats from finding weeds to eat.

The goats seemed to snicker as the boys set out to make them stronger.

Some of the smaller children jumped into the farm truck (I still call it a moving crate!) and went with the Farmer with the funny hat to get something else to help fix the problem.

The children could not contain their excitement...

VOCABULARY WORDS

Use the glossary in the back of the book to find the meaning of each word or phrase:

farm truck _____

_____

tools _____

_____

sneaking _____

_____

predator _____

_____

ACTIVITY: DRAW THE MISSING PARTS:

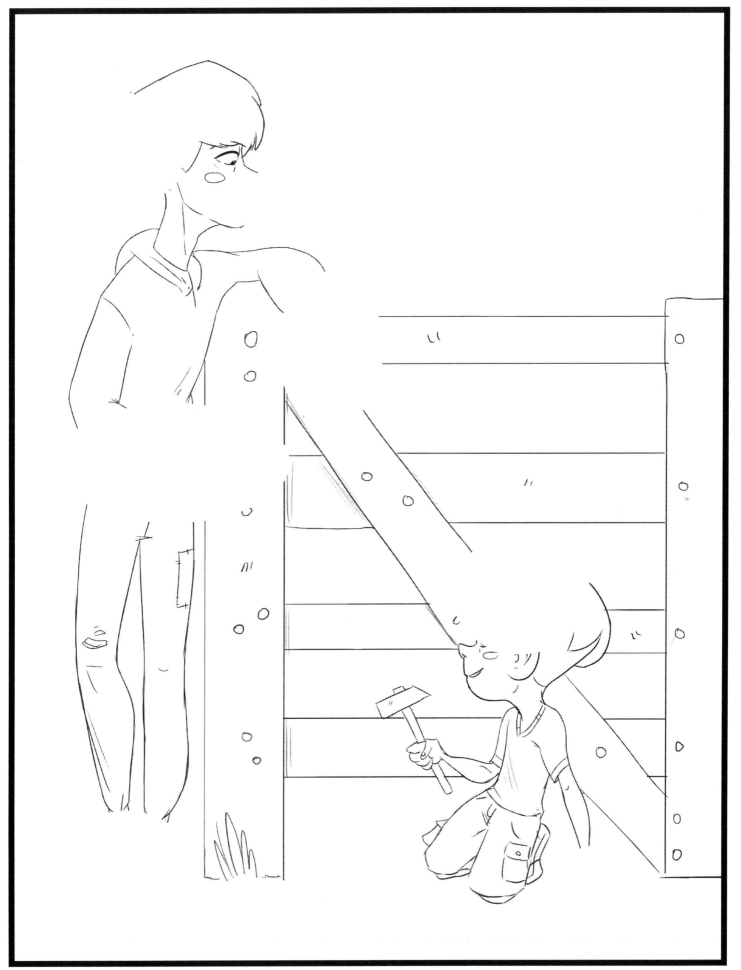

The farm truck came back in a cloud of dust. The children jumped out of the farm truck very excited. Then I saw what they brought with them. I could not believe my eyes! They looked like the coyotes I could barely see the night before, only they were white.

I did not like the looks of them. I liked the chickens, even Robbie. I liked Belle. I liked the goats. I liked the sheep. But,

I did not like these big coyotes!

One was really big and one was small. I did not know why the children were so happy.

One of the children said: "Come here Pippa, meet Simon and Salty, our new dogs!" **Dogs?** Those furry coyotes were really dogs? Simon was so, so big! He was so big the little ones were climbing all over him. He just stood there looking like he was smiling and enjoying everything.

He looked very happy! They said Simon would stay with the goats and the sheep and protect them from the coyotes. He seemed too nice to fight coyotes, but he is much bigger.

I started to like Simon and felt much safer.

VOCABULARY WORDS

Use the glossary in the back of the book to find the meaning of each word or phrase:

livestock guardian dog _____

_____

herding dog _____

_____

herd _____

_____

combine _____

_____

ACTIVITY: RESEARCH PAGE

RESEARCH HERDING DOGS AND TELL ABOUT THEIR USE WITH LIVESTOCK ON FARMS:

Salty, though, was a different story. Salty seemed to be mean and bossy. She seemed to think it was her job to make all the animals go wherever she wanted them to go. I did not like that.

The Farmer with the funny hat opened a gate, and gave Salty a command that I did not understand. As soon as he whistled, Salty made all of the sheep and the goats,

even Garrett, Gabby, and George,

walk through the gate. They then went all the way to the back of the pasture near where Belle was grazing. Then Salty and the Farmer with the funny hat came back together, like they were working together.

Salty looked very happy. It turns out the sheep and the goats were very happy too because Salty herded them to the tastiest and freshest grass on the farm!

It made me wonder if being mean and bossy is why she is here.

VOCABULARY WORDS

Use the glossary in the back of the book to find the meaning of each word or phrase:

command _____

_____

whistle _____

_____

working _____

_____

bossy _____

_____

ACTIVITY: CAN YOU DRAW IT?
DRAW A PICTURE OF SALTY HERDING THE SHEEP:

After staring at the purple and orange sky for a while, and eating again, I was very tired. I was almost asleep when I realized that I was not scared like I had been the night before.

What changed?

Simon was close by, always protecting the farm. That is what was different. Simon was very gentle, and I knew he would keep us safe and would fiercely fight off any predators.

I then remembered the place where I lived before I came to this farm.

I was sad for all the pigs there.

I am so happy that I was chosen to come here, to this place that is now home.

VOCABULARY WORDS

Use the glossary in the back of the book to find the meaning of each word or phrase:

changed _____

_____

gentle _____

_____

thankful _____

_____

live _____

_____

ACTIVITY: DRAW THE MISSING PARTS:

Today, I am thankful that the chickens get to live like real chickens and run around.

I am thankful that Belle gets to be a real cow and eat grass.

I am thankful that the goats get to run and play. I am thankful that the sheep get to live like real sheep.

I am thankful for Simon that keeps us safe.

I am even thankful for Salty, and even though she still irritates me sometimes, she helps the flocks and herds find the best pastures. I trust that if the Farmer with the funny hat thinks we are all needed and belong here, then Salty must also be important and belong here.

I am happy that at this farm I get to live like a real pig.

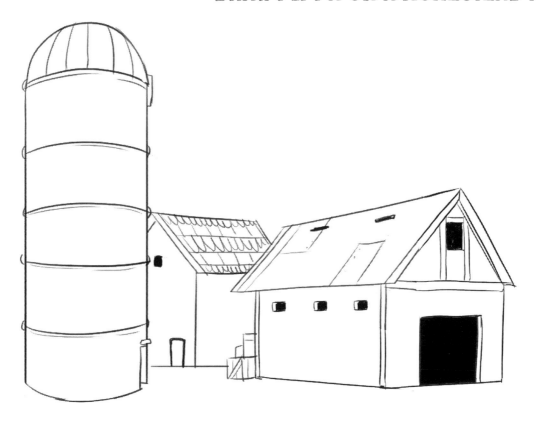

DRAW PIPPA ON A HOMESTEAD FARM

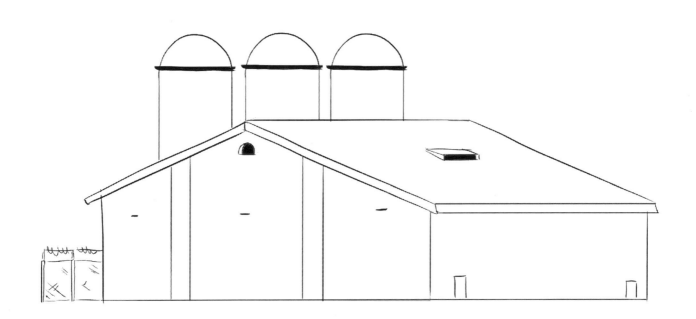

DRAW PIPPA ON AN INDUSTRIAL FARM

VOCABULARY WORDS

Use the glossary in the back of the book to find the meaning of each word or phrase:

supposed _____

_____

important _____

_____

belong _____

_____

job _____

_____

ACTIVITY: RESEARCH PAGE

RESEARCH FARM SAFETY. TELL ABOUT THE WAYS TO PROTECT ANIMALS AND KEEP PEOPLE SAFE:

_____

_____

_____

_____

_____

_____

_____

_____

_____

_____

_____

_____

_____

_____

_____

_____

_____

_____

_____

It seems like all of us on this farm are here for a reason. Like we are all *really* supposed to be here. Like there is something really important for each of us to do.

We do not have to do anything like anyone else, because then we would not be doing what we are supposed to be doing. We do not have to worry what anyone else thinks about us.

We just need to be
who we were each made to be.

Except for Salty. Salty's job is to worry about where everybody else is supposed to be, that must be why she is here.

And the Farmer with the funny hat, he knows where everyone should always be, and what they should do, and why they are here. He knows our needs and he takes care of us.

I now understand that even I,
a pig with a real name,
must be really, really important.

ESSAY

Write a paragraph about how the animals all
work together on a farm:

_____

_____

_____

_____

_____

_____

_____

_____

_____

_____

ACTIVITY: CAN YOU DRAW IT?
DRAW A PICTURE OF YOUR FAMILY ON A FARM:

GLOSSARY

4H: an agricultural group or club for children that features hands-on learning.

acorns: the fruit from the oak tree which is a favorite natural food of swine.

activity: using energy in lively action or work.

agriculture: the production of crops, livestock, or poultry.

alfalfa: a perennial flowering plant that resembles clover with clusters of small bluish-purple flowers. Alfalfa is a favorite feed for dairy cows.

barn: a large building for storing hay, grain, etc., and often for housing livestock.

battery farm: a farm on which chickens or calves are kept very close together in small boxes, crates, or cages.

belong: to be part of a group.

boar: a male swine.

bossy: ordering someone around in an irritating way.

bovine: beef or dairy cattle.

breakfast: a meal that is eaten in the morning.

bull: an adult male animal of the bovine or cattle family.

buried: to place in the ground and cover with earth.

changed: becoming different.

chicken: a domestic fowl bred for its flesh or eggs.

chicken coop: an enclosure, shed, small barn, or pen, in which beds are built for female fowl to lay their eggs. The chicken coop will have bars or wires to protect the chickens at night.

combine: a tractor type machine used to harvest grains.

command: to give orders to someone or something, such as a herding dog.

concrete: a mixture of cement, sand, stone, and water that hardens into stone.

corn meal: a coarse flour ground from dried corn soaked in an alkaline solution.

cow: a female breed of bovine that is kept on farms and used to produce milk or meat.

coyotes: also known as a prairie wolf; a predatory canine mammal, related to the wolf but smaller in size.

crate: a small metal cage with concrete floors used to confine animals.

dairy cow: cattle cows (also called dairy cattle or milk cows) with larger udders and less muscle mass, bred to produce large quantities of milk, from which dairy products are made.

discussion: a conversation or debate to find a solution to a matter.

dreaming: images that pass through the mind while sleeping.

everywhere: in all places.

ewe: a female sheep.

excited: very strong uncontrolled emotion.

experience: wisdom that is gained by what a person has felt, seen, and done.

explore: to examine or investigate; to travel to or into unfamiliar or unknown regions.

factory farming: large farms whose purpose is profit with animals kept indoors and/or on concrete lots with restricted mobility.

farm truck: a pickup or flatbed truck used for hauling farm animals and equipment.

farther: a physical distance greater than the beginning point.

feed lots: a small area, usually without grass, where cattle are confined and fed high-concentrate feed to fatten them.

fence: a structure usually made of wood or metal that surrounds a piece of land providing a barrier to keep animals in and predators out.

field: a meadow or area of open land.

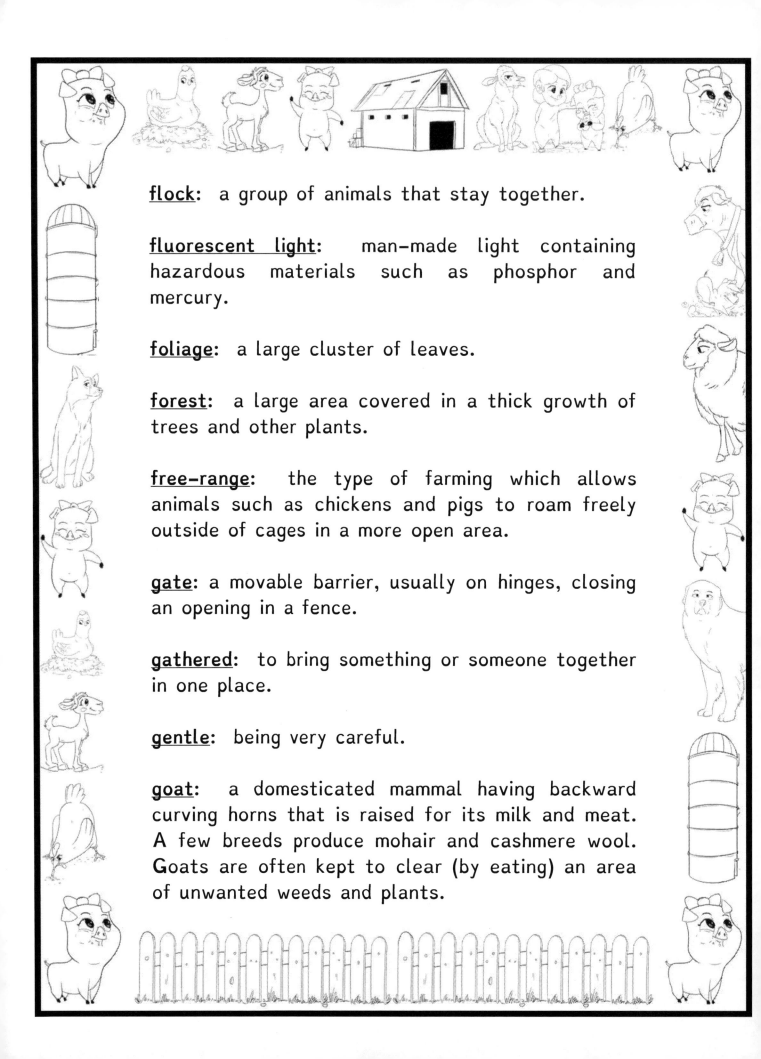

flock: a group of animals that stay together.

fluorescent light: man-made light containing hazardous materials such as phosphor and mercury.

foliage: a large cluster of leaves.

forest: a large area covered in a thick growth of trees and other plants.

free-range: the type of farming which allows animals such as chickens and pigs to roam freely outside of cages in a more open area.

gate: a movable barrier, usually on hinges, closing an opening in a fence.

gathered: to bring something or someone together in one place.

gentle: being very careful.

goat: a domesticated mammal having backward curving horns that is raised for its milk and meat. A few breeds produce mohair and cashmere wool. Goats are often kept to clear (by eating) an area of unwanted weeds and plants.

grains: small, hard, dry seeds, such as wheat, rye, legumes, beans, and soybeans, harvested for human or animal consumption.

groundwater: underground water that has leaked through soil layers and bedrock.

harvest: the season, usually in Autumn, when ripened crops are gathered.

hatchery: a place where eggs are hatched under artificial conditions.

hay: grass or other plants, such as clover or alfalfa, which is cut and dried, and then baled for feed.

heifer: a young cow over one year old that has not produced a calf.

hen: the female of the domestic chicken or fowl.

herd: a group of cattle that live together in a flock.

herding dog: a type of pastoral dog, also known as a working dog, that is trained in herding animals with the sound of whistles or word commands.

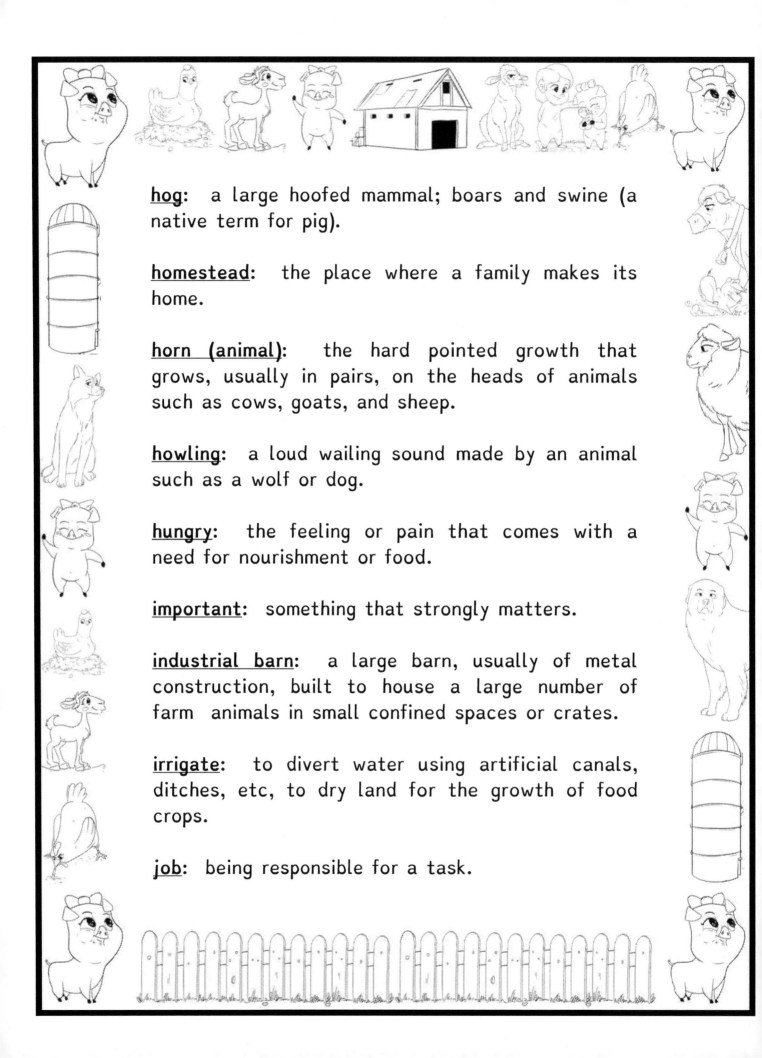

hog: a large hoofed mammal; boars and swine (a native term for pig).

homestead: the place where a family makes its home.

horn (animal): the hard pointed growth that grows, usually in pairs, on the heads of animals such as cows, goats, and sheep.

howling: a loud wailing sound made by an animal such as a wolf or dog.

hungry: the feeling or pain that comes with a need for nourishment or food.

important: something that strongly matters.

industrial barn: a large barn, usually of metal construction, built to house a large number of farm animals in small confined spaces or crates.

irrigate: to divert water using artificial canals, ditches, etc, to dry land for the growth of food crops.

job: being responsible for a task.

kid: a young goat.

live: to exist in a place where you have made your home.

livestock: non-domesticated animals, such as sheep, goats, cows, and horses, kept or raised on a farm or ranch.

livestock guardian dog: a pastoral dog bred to stay with livestock to protect the animals from predators.

manure: animal waste from stables or barnyards which can be recycled into fertilizer.

milk: a white liquid produced by females for nourishment. The milk of cows, goats, or other animals is used as food or to produce butter, cheese, and other dairy products.

milking parlor: a building or barn where milk is taken from cows.

mobile hen house: a chicken coop which can be moved around the yard or farm to allow the fowl access to fresh grass and food.

natural light: light that comes from the sun.

normal: something that is usual, average, or expected.

noticed: to observe or pay attention to something.

occasionally: every once in a while.

opinion: your views, beliefs, or ideas about a subject.

organic farming: farms that rely on the natural earth to grow food and animals. The use of synthetic fertilizers, artificial hormones, herbicides, and pesticides are generally prohibited.

pasture raised: the type of farming which allows animals to live outdoors where they are allowed access to natural foods.

pesticide: a harmful chemical used to kill unwanted animals or plants.

picnic: a meal that is eaten outdoors.

pig: any wild or domestic swine; the animal that produces pork meat such as ham, pepperoni, or sausage.

plank: a long, flat piece of timber, thicker than a board, which on a farm is used for chickens to access the coop.

poultry: birds such as chickens and ducks that are kept on farms in order to produce eggs and meat.

predator: an animal that hunts and attacks others for food.

protect: to defend or guard from attack, invasion, injury, or danger.

proud: being pleased or satisfied with an accomplishment.

ram: a male sheep.

ranch: any large farm for the growing of a particular kind of livestock or crop.

rooster: the male of domestic chicken or fowl.

seemed: to give the impression or appearance that something exists.

shear: to remove the fleece from the animal with cutting tools.

sheep: a farm animal with a thick coat of wool.

sneaking: being secretive about something.

soil: earth, ground, or land.

sow: an adult female swine.

squawk: to utter a loud, harsh cry, from a rooster, duck, or other fowl when frightened.

stressed: to worry or to be concerned about something enough to cause unrest.

supposed: claiming to be true.

thankful: being grateful and glad.

thistle: a prickly weed with purple flower heads.

through: to go in one side and out another side.

tools: an instrument or piece of equipment used to help with a job or task.

tractor: a powerful motor-driven vehicle with large, heavy treads, used for pulling farm machinery, other vehicles, etc.

trouble: to cause disorder, discomfort, or pain to a situation.

trough: a long, narrow box used for holding water or feed for animals.

weed: any plant that grows wild and will choke out cultivated plants.

whistle: a high-pitched musical sound made by blowing air through the teeth, used in giving commands to herding dogs.

wonderful: a feeling of great quality that gives happiness.

wool: the soft thick hair or fleece grown on sheep and goats which can be used to make clothes.

working: performing a task or job to benefit others.

About The Author:

Mark Apple grew up on a family farm in McCordsville, Indiana. Upon graduating from high school, he was at a crossroads on deciding which career path to take: follow his roots and pursue a life in agriculture, or follow a passion for music. Music won out. Mark graduated from Anderson University with a degree in Music Industry/Marketing, which led to a 15 year career working in Nashville, TN for various Country and Christian music artists. However, farming was always in the blood. As a side business, Mark established a herd of beef cattle and started raising grass-fed beef.

Following the death of his father, Mark moved back to the family farm in Indiana, becoming the 5th generation to farm the land. He successfully converted it from a conventional grain farm to a 100% grass-fed dairy and beef farm. The farm also had pastured poultry, occasionally sheep and goats, and trained working dogs. One of the most fulfilling aspects of the farm was having groups of children from various backgrounds visit the farm where Mark and Nora enjoyed the opportunity to educate about just how amazing, special, and healthy our food could be when the animals were allowed to live and eat as they were created. That passion to educate on the benefits of natural farming is the reason for this book. Mark and Nora have now retired from the farm, and are pursuing various ministry and mission projects at home and abroad.

About The Publisher:

Our family has known Mark and Nora, and the Apple family, for many years. We even lived and worked at the Apple's farm for a few years helping with the animals and managing the farm store. Our children enjoyed playing in the lush green pastures where, as parents, we were not concerned about harm from chemicals. Their experiences enhanced our homeschooling and heightened first-hand educational learning. We are excited to be a part of encouraging the next generation in natural farming practices.

Sarah Janisse Brown

Made in the USA
Middletown, DE
06 February 2025

70626561R00084